MY LIFE ALONG THE EDGE
(And Back Again)

Eugene Montgomery

Copyright © 2016 by Eugene and Myla Montgomery

All rights reserved. Except for appropriate use in critical reviews or works of scholarship, no part of this work may be reproduced or transmitted in any form, electronic or mechanical, including photocopy, recording or any information storage and retrieval system without the written permission of the publisher.

Cover Designed by: Myla Montgomery and Ron Snowden
Edited by: Myla Montgomery and Ron Snowden

My Life Along the Edge – And Back Again –
First edition, 2016
ISBN# 978-0-692-79855-3

Printed in the U. S. A.
The copyright laws of Title 17 United States Code apply.

ACKNOWLEDGEMENTS

A special thanks to my wife, Myla Montgomery, for helping me put this book together and for all her encouragement and editing skills. Thank you to my departed Mother, Eloise Montgomery, for being my rock, my best friend and for her guidance to help me be the person I am today. Thank you to all of my friends who persuaded me to write this book and for all their encouragement. Thanks to Lee Clark and to his family for helping this little black boy survive growing up in the South (even though Mr. Clark was a white man).

ABOUT THE AUTHOR

Eugene Montgomery was born on October 11, 1941 in Eutawville, South Carolina to sharecropper parents  who picked tobacco, cotton and corn in the South. With various jobs at Amtrak, being a New York City cab driver and just growing up in the South, he has always been happy to have lived passed the age of 25 and wanted to share his life stories with everyone. After living in several locations around the perimeter of the United States, Eugene now resides near Seattle, WA with his wife, Myla.

TABLE OF CONTENTS

GROWING UP IN SOUTH CAROLINA — 7
- The Day I Left My Body — 9
- Lee Clark Sold us Land — 11
- My Dad, The Sawmill and the Snake — 11
- Arthur Blunt, Ruby and Amos — 13
- Tobacco Worm — 16
- Sundays in South Carolina — 19
- My Family and Storms — 20
- The Ghosts are Walking — 22
- Midnight Ride to New York City — 25

MOVING TO NEW YORK CITY — 29
- Living in the Middle of Gangs — 29
- Moving by Yankee Stadium — 32
- Joining a Band — 34
- Moving out of my Sister's House — 37
- Being a New York City Cab Driver — 38
- Pelham One Two — 39
- Caught in the Middle of Riots — 45
- Pick up from LaGuardia Airport — 46
- Picking up the lady from Macy's — 49
- Three Kids with Shooting — 50
- Getting Kicked — 51
- Two Ladies with Briefcases in Central Park — 52
- The Bellevue Hospital Pickup — 53

    My Last Cab Drive   54
    Cab Stories Wrap Up   56

MOVING TO FLORIDA & CALIFORNIA   59
    Getting a Job with the Railroad   59

TRAIN STORIES   65
    Can You Fly?   65
    Toilet Flushing Problems   66
    Too Hot or Too Cold   67
    Military Guy Gets Free Booze   69
    Bats in the Attic   69
    Jalapeño Peppers and Bombs   70
    Seeing Eye Parrot   72
    Ferret Surprise   73
    Native Americans Have an Uprising   74
    Meeting Martha Stewart and
        Other Celebrities   74

EXCITING TIMES IN CALIFORNIA   77
    Starting Monty Import/Export Business   77
    Cool Breeze   81
    Girlfriend starts Using Heroin   83
    Turmoil at Home   84
    House Gets Shot Up   86
    Girlfriend Leaves   88
    Leaving California for Seattle   89

LIFE CALMS DOWN	91
How I Met My Wife	91
Finding My Birth Certificate	94
Closing Thoughts	96

Chapter One

GROWING UP IN SOUTH CAROLINA

I was born on October 11, 1941 to Eloise and Isaac Montgomery in a small house in Eutawville, SC by a midwife. At least that's what I've been told as we still to this day haven't been able to locate a birth certificate.

I had 8 siblings – 5 brothers and 3 sisters. Harry was the oldest, then Dan, followed by Mae Kathryn, Isaac, Jr., me, Leroy, George, Rebecca and Ella Mae. Isaac, Jr. died when he was very young not even in school. Ella Mae also died when she was young from blood poisoning.

She fell down on a stick when she was playing and it turned into gangrene.

Eutawville was a very tiny town of maybe a thousand people. We had no stoplights and one movie theater. During that time, the movie theater had two entrances – one for the white people and one for the black people. Inside, the whites sat on one side and the blacks on the other with a wall in between us. There were drinking fountains for whites and drinking fountains for blacks. And to this day in 2016, there is still a cemetery for whites and one for blacks.

We use to have a farmer's picnic every August. All the farmers would bring in their crops to sell. The streets were lined with tables and tents from farmers in the area. I think it was similar to our present day Farmer's Markets. That was when Eutawville was really booming.

A house was being built for us to live in Eutawville. So while they were building this house, we moved to Vance, SC just a short distance from Eutawville. This house was owned by Lee Clark who turned out to be a big influence in my life.

My sister, Mae, woke us up early one morning telling us to get up, get up – the house is on fire. They think the fire was due to faulty wiring. This was the first house I lived in with electricity. All my personal records and pictures were destroyed in that fire so that's why I don't have my birth certificate. But as it turns out neither does the State of South Carolina – but more on that later.

THE DAY I LEFT MY BODY

In those days, we had to make up our own fun and games. There were no electronic games during this time.

In the 1950's, my Mother worked for Lee Clark, a white man. He was a very important influence in my life. He had a son named Lee Junior. Mr. Clark took Lee Jr. and me fishing sometimes because he owned many boats.

Lee Junior (Lee Clark's only boy) told me when you come to my house come to the front door not the back door because typically white people in South Carolina never wanted a black person to come to the front door. His kids would come to my house and sit down and eat with us and we did the same at his house. Lee Clark was a good man.

One day, Lee Jr. got his bicycle out and we went up to the top of the hill and came speeding down toward the store and just before we were about to hit the store building, we'd jam the brakes in order to swing the bike around to see who could get the closest to the building without hitting it.

We kept getting closer and closer and then it was my time. Again, I came flying down the hill really fast and I waited too long to hit the brakes and went flying head first into the side of the brick store building. I busted my forehead open. I could see myself on the ground as I was going far up into the clouds. I could see my body on the ground struggling to get up.

I came down really fast from the clouds when I came crashing back into my body. Blood was gushing everywhere. As I got up I staggered into the store, pressed the key down on the cash register and took the dollar bills out of the drawer and put them to my head to stop the bleeding. Notice I didn't take the coins; I went for the big bills because I thought that would stop the bleeding. They rushed me to the doctor in Holly Hill, SC which was 8 miles away. We didn't have a doctor in Eutawville where I lived. Mr. Clark drove the car really fast – but I must have passed out as I don't remember that ride. When I woke up we were back in the car and going back home.

All the dollars I damaged my Mother had to pay back to the store.

That's the time I knew I had an out of body experience as I went way up to the clouds and could look down at me on the ground. I never tried that trick again after that. It took that to cure us of that one. Every time my Mother saw me on a bicycle, she asked me "you're not going to go slamming into the store again are you?" I promised her I would never do that again. And I still have the scar on my face to remind me of this adventure.

LEE CLARK SOLD US LAND

Lee Clark sold us four acres of land in Eutawville for $100 an acre. I asked my Dad, "Why do we need 4 acres of land?" And he said, "You'll understand one day." We built a house, a chicken coop (because we raised chickens), and a pig pen. The only thing I can figure out as to why we had our own house was that it was better for us to own our own home instead of being sharecroppers and living in someone else's house. When you were sharecroppers, you had to do what the owners said. If they wanted us to pick cotton or tobacco or whatever – that's what we had to do. And they could kick you out of the house whenever they wanted. So it was better to own your own home so we wouldn't get kicked out.

Working in the fields was terrible work. It was the hot, sticky south and being out in the hot sun all day was exhausting. While we were working in the fields, sometimes a plane would fly over real low and spray the fields. They were spraying for bow weevil, mosquitoes and who knows what. They always told us it wouldn't hurt us – I don't know about that. Two of my siblings and I all had cancer and I can't help but think that had something to do with it.

MY DAD, THE SAWMILL AND THE SNAKE

My Dad was able to buy that four acres of land because he worked in the sawmill. As he was wrapping the chain around a log to pull it back to the sawmill, there was a rattlesnake under the log. It bit my Dad but as he was trying to pull away from the snake, the snake attached himself to my Dad's arm. So my Dad stepped on the snake with his foot and pulled and pulled until the snake snapped in half and killed him that way. He took the head of the snake out of his arm and threw it on the ground. Then they took him to Holly Hill Hospital (about 8 miles away) to treat him.

So when my father's brother, Dave, came home as he was telling my mother the story of what had happened, there was a car that pulled up in the yard. My Dad was in the backseat.

The man opened the door and said that "Boy (my Dad's nickname) would be alright."

I always remember that night the "ghosts" walked again. I was so afraid because my dad was sick and the KKK was riding their horses by our house. As always my Mother would blow the lamp out because we didn't have electricity. I know it was in the summer because we picked cotton the next day.

My Mom boiled some concoction and had my Dad drink it to help him heal. It was some kind of tea. Then my Mother asked for the Root Doctor. Everyone in Carolina believed in the Root Doctor. He was some crazy looking man who came over and shook some beads and said some words. He put his hand on my dad and made crazy sounds – but as a little boy I didn't understand. The Root Doctor said "He will be alright now, Mrs. Montgomery." My mother walked him to the door, put her hand in her apron pocket and gave him something.

After a few days, my Dad explained to all of us how the snake got him. He said as he was hooking up a log to be pulled back to the mill, he reached his arm around the log. He thought he had stuck himself on something, but it was the rattlesnake that got him. As he pulled his arm out, the snake was still stuck in his arm. He grabbed it by the head and killed it.

This whole ordeal left my Dad's left side partially paralyzed and weak from this point on. That is when I think he started drinking heavily because he couldn't work and help my Mother. Lee Clark let my dad do some work for him. He had a fish house so he would catch a lot of fish. My Mom and Dad would clean them for him. That was a nasty job. I don't think my Dad ever went back to work at the Mill.

ARTHUR BLUNT, RUBY AND AMOS

My Mother worked for Ruby (a white woman) who had a husband named Amos. Ruby ran the store that was owned by a man named Arthur Blunt. Arthur Blunt was the scariest man I ever met. I always looked down on the ground whenever I was around him. I could feel his stare.

Arthur Blunt was in charge of all the boat races every

Sunday. He had a lot of cabins along the water that people could rent to stay in while they were attending the boat races. Every Sunday we would go and watch the boat races. For a kid, that was fun. We had to walk from Eutawville to Eutaw Springs which seemed like 5 miles to us but it was actually only half that. We went there to watch the boat races.

Arthur was messing around with both Ruby and her sister, Molly (she was the baby of the two sisters). I went to see my Mother one day while she was working for Ruby. I had to pass outside right by the bedroom because I had to go to the back door, of course. That put me right passed Arthur Blunt's bedroom. That's when I saw Molly in bed with him.

When I told my Mother what I saw, she whispered to me "you didn't see what you thought you saw."

I could see in her eyes that she was afraid of what I just saw and told her. She told me to go back home, do my lessons and forget about what I just saw. She sent me back to the house a different way so I didn't have to go passed the bedroom window again. She was just trying to protect me. Back at the house I didn't tell my other siblings about what I saw because I didn't want them to get involved with what must have been a scary situation.

My Mother and Father would always go out by the pig pen and talk when they didn't want the kids to know what they were talking about. When my Father got home that afternoon that's what they did. So I figured they were talking about what I saw.

Amos (Ruby's husband) told me that he was going away for a while and when he came back he was going to take all the black kids fishing. We would always look forward to that. Amos went away but he never came back. The next thing we heard was that his body was found in the pigpen. They told us the pigs ate him. Two policemen came to the house one day and asked where my Mother was. My Dad told me to go get my Mother. When my Mother came out she was drying her hands on her apron.

The police asked my mother "When was the last time you saw Amos and was he upset?"

My mother said "I know when my husband is upset but I don't know when Amos is upset."

The police said "We found his body today in the pig pen and the pigs ate him. There was a hole in the back of his head. He must have been put in a freezer or something as it looked like he'd been dead for a while and then put in the pig pen."

She said "He was supposed to take the kids fishing when he came back. So they are going to be upset that they can't go."

After the police left, my mother told me to go play because she didn't want me to hear what they were talking about.

I took a stick and went out to our pigpen and started

hitting the pigs and asking them, "Which one of you ate Mr. Amos?"

I thought it was one of our pigs that ate him. My mother and father wondered what was wrong with that kid of ours that was hitting the pigs with a stick. After I told them what I was doing, they told me it was in a different pig pen and not ours.

Two years later Ruby married Arthur Blunt – the same guy who she used to work for at the store. I still thought he was responsible for killing Amos her first husband since I caught him messing around with the two sisters Ruby and Molly.

TOBACCO WORM

I must tell you why we called my cousin, Moses Brisban, "Tobacco Worm." My mother and her sister took a lot of kids to harvest tobacco each summer in North Carolina. Moses was one of the kids that went along. My mother was responsible for all of the children. All the girls slept on one side of the house and all of the boys on the other side of house. We were sharecroppers.

The farm that we were working on let us fill up the barn by 2 pm and then we would go and work for another farmer.

Moses was the fastest tobacco picker that I have ever seen. His hands were so fast. And that's why we called him Tobacco Worm. We got paid $20 per person for one barn of tobacco and $20 for the second barn. To make

$40 for a kid in the '50's was a lot of money. To fill the two barns, it took us all day long with 6 pickers and 6 stringers. The pickers would pick the tobacco and the stringers strung it up to hang in the barn to dry.

One day, Moses (Tobacco Worm), and the rest of the kids had gone to town to buy clothes for the coming school year. After we had shopped, we were on the way back to the place where we were staying. We stopped off at a club because there were a lot of black kids outside. So we decided to stop and go inside to see all the new people that we did not know. As we entered the club, there was a young lady dressed up in red sitting at the counter. All of our attention was on her but she had other ideas.

She and Moses hit it off right away. So my other cousin and I danced with the rest of the ladies. We had fun with the girls and then it was time to go. I could not find Moses and I told my cousin I couldn't find him. I decided to check the car and there he was in the backseat with the woman in red "getting busy." I was kind of shocked but was glad for him. That was Friday night and I patted him on the back telling him how lucky he was.

But we found out later he was not so lucky because Saturday he slept all day and Sunday he got sick, Monday we went back to work picking tobacco and while we were picking, Moses got sicker and sicker. We rushed him to a hospital where he died on Wednesday. We were trying to find the lady in the red dress but no one in the club said that they knew her. The doctor wanted to make sure that whatever he had that woman probably had the same thing. That was very hard on my mother because she felt she had lost a son. My mother then had to tell Moses' mother who was back in South Carolina about what had happened to her son.

I will never forget the doctor took all of the clothes that I was wearing when I brought Moses in the hospital and burned them. My cousin's and everyone's clothes who touched Moses as he was getting sick were burned. White stuff was coming out of his mouth like a sick dog foaming at the mouth. When he leaned on me, all the white stuff went onto my shirt. I was given a hospital jacket of some kind to put on and they burned my clothes. Everyone Moses had touched, their clothes were burned. I never knew what kind of sickness he had. All I know is my friend died and I didn't feel so sad. I didn't feel so sad because I felt one day he would come back. As a kid that's the way you think.

My mother took the boys outside and asked each of us, "Did you touch that young lady."

I said, "Only Moses touched that young lady."

"Are you sure?" my mom quizzed.

"Yes, I am sure." I said.

"All right if you say so," she said. She studied me for a while turned on her heel and walked away. I didn't know what the doctor told her. She never told us because maybe we were too young to know. She read the Bible and spent a lot of time with the girls and the boys spent a lot of time with the men who had gone on the trip. The ladies had control of the girls and men had all the control of the boys and that's the way it was.

My dad stayed at home because he was having his problem with alcohol and that was the last year that I went to work on the tobacco farm. Up until that year as long as I could remember we picked tobacco in the summer. All the money we made, we bought clothes for the following school year.

SUNDAYS IN SOUTH CAROLINA

My father had two brothers, Dave and Shula. Dave was the oldest of the three. Shula was the baby and my father was in the middle. Each Sunday they would go to Spring Hill Baptist Church. Dave was a deacon and my father was just a member and so was his brother Shula.

It seemed like we would sit for hours listening to the preacher holler at us. And the only bible was the one the preacher had so they only preached what they wanted you to know.

My father would make fun that each Sunday the preacher would come by to eat at each one of our houses. Of course, it was chicken because everyone always had chicken on Sunday and fish on Friday. Then he would go home and eat more chicken.

My sister and her friends would be doing their hair. The

boys would be outside playing checkers but sometimes cards or climbing and playing in my tree house. That's the way it was on Sunday – very lazy and laid back.

MY FAMILY AND STORMS

    I have asked my sister, Mae, how she got to New York. I'm not sure what she said but it had something to do with being married and moving with her husband. My brother, Dan, went to North Carolina to work for Daniel Construction Company building one of the first freeways that came almost to my town. I was so proud of him. He smoked a cigar and drank scotch whiskey because he could afford it. He was a big shot because no one in my family could afford to drink scotch whiskey but Dan did.

    By this time, my brother, Harry, enlisted in the Air Force. I don't know when it happened but he came home one day and had on his uniform. He also was driving a car that you could stand up on the sideboard. As he rode around the neighborhood, we all would ride on the sideboards of his car. That was the first car that we had in our family. Everyone was saying that night how glad they were to have him leaving South Carolina to get away from all the problems with the ghosts, etc.

    We all gathered around because another storm was coming in. It seemed like there were always storms in South Carolina. They were sometimes so bad that we had to board up all the windows especially when the hurricanes came through.

Harry parked the car up along side of the house. We all went inside and hoped for the best. As a kid, I was just scared. The house would just shake. It felt like the house was going to blow away. Of course, you always had to go to the bathroom when this happened. My mother would put a bucket in the kitchen so we would not have to go outside to use the outhouse which was our bathroom.

For those of you who don't know what an outhouse is, let me explain. In those times, houses didn't have indoor plumbing or running water. So you would have to go fetch water from the pump outside and bring it in. You would also have to go outside to the bathroom. Usually a big hole was dug in the ground at an out of way place away from the house. Then a small four by four house was put on top of it. Inside was a place to sit and on that sitting place was at least one hole and sometimes two holes where you would have to sit and "do your business." Whenever the big hole got too full, we'd have to dig another hole someplace else and move the small outhouse there. The first hole would just be covered up – great fertilizer!

When there was a storm, the night always seemed the longest but the ghosts didn't walk during a storm. That was one good thing about storms – never having to worry about the ghosts. The lightning would flash and it would light the whole house up. You could hear everyone's gasps from my sister and brother when the lightning and thunder sounded. My mother was always the calm one saying it will be all right. You will be just fine. My dad would just pat whoever's head was near to him saying you will be fine – "The storm will blow over soon." To a kid, soon was not fast enough.

Boom the thunder would roar. The lightning flashed all night long. It sounded like a bomb had gone off and then the lightning would flash again. The wind was blowing so hard that some water got into the house. My mother would put a blanket up to the window to make sure the house would not get too cold. I heard someone say "I have to go to the bathroom." Mom or dad would get a flashlight and walk the kids to the kitchen to use the bucket. It never failed, it always happened.

The next morning as we walked to school, that's all we talked about – the storm last night and how scared everyone was. The next big scare is the "ghosts." The storms came only once in a while but the ghosts were always there.

THE GHOSTS ARE WALKING

It was scary for a little black kid growing up in the South in the '40's and '50's. As a little boy my mother used to tell me "Don't play in the woods at night because the ghosts was walking." Down south the ghost is always walking at least that's what the kids believe. Let me tell you about the ghost each night in a black neighborhood.

The "ghosts", of course, were the KKK dressed up in their white sheets. The Klan would ride through on their horses with torch in hand looking to see if any house had lights. I guess they were looking for any black kid or adult who maybe didn't make it home in time and was still outside. They were looking for a little excitement.

There was no electricity in our house. We had lamps in each room to light the house up. So when the Klan came by, mom or dad would blow the lamps out to make the house dark. I remember hiding behind my mother when this would happen being scared to death. I can't remember how old I was but young enough to be very scared. I don't believe a black man was allowed to have guns but I'm not sure otherwise, we might have been able to fight back.

My cousin, Jeff Montgomery, and I were playing one day and three white boys were walking towards us. Jeff said it looks like it's going to be trouble and he was right.

One of the other boys said "are you boys lost?"

"No," Jeff replied "Are you?"

And then a car pulls up. The man in the car called out to the other boys. "Are you guys okay?"

"Yes, Dad" he said.

"Then go back to the house, your Mother is waiting for you." the driver said.

One of the boys said in a soft voice, "Lucky bastard."

Jeff said, "Yeah, lucky bastard."

The three boys ran off in the direction of their house. The car rolled down the street very slow as Jeff and I kept walking.

"What was that all about?" I asked him.

"That white boy never liked me," he said.

I looked at him with a grin on my face. "Do you think he likes me?"

"No." Jeff said, "He might be one of those guys who ride the horse. I wouldn't be surprised"

Another time after Jeff and I got done playing baseball, we were coming out of the store and walked into the boy who said lucky bastard to Jeff. He tried to block our path. The lady behind the counter called him Billy. She said "Billy, get out of the way." This boy was getting on my nerves – he had already gotten on Jeff's nerves. That was the last time I saw Jeff in South Carolina. I was told that he had gone off to work but I never asked where.

I remember one day Lee Clark Junior had taken me into the woods to play. Some men riding a horse came up to Lee Junior and me.

One of the men said to Lee Junior "did this boy bring you out here in the woods?" Remember, Lee Junior, was a white boy.

Lee Junior said "No, I brought him."

"Are you sure?" The man said.

"Yes, I'm sure," Junior replied.

I didn't look up at the men but one of them said to get out of the woods. Lee Jr. took my hand and said come on and I followed him out of the woods. I didn't look back to see what the men were doing I just got out of the woods. I told my mother and father the story and I could see the look on their face.

I didn't know what they were thinking but the next thing I know I'm getting put in a car in the middle of the night.

MY MIDNIGHT RIDE TO NEW YORK CITY

All I remember is that it was dark outside; my mother came in my room and woke me up and said "Batman, get up." (Batman was my nickname because Mom sent me to the store with a grocery list one time which I threw away. I came home with a box of BB Bat suckers instead – hence the Batman nickname.) She was putting my clothes on real fast and saying a lot of things I didn't understand. What I remember her saying is that you will thank me one day for this. As a young boy I didn't understand it.

They put me in Lee Clark's car since we didn't own one. Mr. Clark drove, my dad was in the front seat and my mom and I were in the back seat. They drove me to Orangeburg and put me on a Greyhound bus that was headed to New York City. My mom said, "Your sister will be there to pick you up and don't get off this bus until you get to New York."

I thought what did I do? Why am I leaving my home? Why does my mother look so afraid? I had lots of questions but no answers.

She walked over and talked to a black lady at the bus station. I don't know what she said to them but the woman bobbed her head up and down and sat me right in front of her. She came onto the bus, gave me a big hug and said "You will be okay. I know you will be all right." She was acting like she was really afraid but I didn't know why. As the bus rolled out of Orangeburg, South Carolina, I kept looking back until there was no more light. That was the last time I saw Orangeburg, South Carolina as a kid.

That was hard for me because my mother was always my best friend. She taught me how to cook, how to respect others, how to make things. I learned all of that from my mother and now I was on my way to a place I had only heard of and that was New York City.

I must have drifted off, because the next thing I know we were stopped at another station. The two ladies sitting behind me said "Young man would you like for me to get something for you? I just shook my head no. The next stop will be New York she told me. "Thank you," I said to her still thinking why did I have to leave home, what did I do or say. As a kid it didn't register but I was on my way to New York City and I was scared. I closed my eyes again from the hard rocking of the bus. The light came on and the bus driver said New York City. The woman that was sitting behind me touched me on the shoulder to make sure I was awake. She whispered to me, "New

York, son."

I looked around and there were lights everywhere I had never seen so many lights as we rolled into the station. My mother said my sister will be there to pick you up. I had a knapsack of some kind and not much clothes. As I got off the bus, the two ladies that were sitting behind me were right behind me. As my sister came over and picked me up, she gave me a big hug and said "are you okay buddy?" Then she talked to the two ladies. One of the women rubbed my head. He was a good kid she told my sister. "Thank you, thank you" my sister said. She took my hand and we walked away.

Chapter Two

MOVING TO NEW YORK CITY

LIVING IN THE MIDDLE OF GANGS IN NEW YORK CITY

My sister and I made some small talk. About what I don't remember but I was glad to see her. I can remember she said that my cousin, Jeff, was in New York and also Louis, his brother. I remember thinking to myself – so that's what happened to cousin Jeff – his parents moved him to New York City, too. His mother and father wanted him out of South Carolina because they were afraid he would be the next one hanging on a tree. So maybe that was why I was here.

We walked for a few blocks and got on something called a subway. Growing up in a small town, I had never even heard of a subway let alone ride in one. This subway was the Lexington Avenuc subway because she lived between Park Avenue and Lexington Avenue on 116th and 117th Street in Harlem.

It was hard getting use to living in the big city since I was brought up in the small town of Eutawville. My sister enrolled me in the PS 126 School. My cousin, Jeff, was also in that school. I learned pretty fast what gangs were all about. If you didn't join one, you were going to be picked on, but my cousin stood up for me.

"Listen to me," Jeff said, "you are in New York City and all these kids want to do is use you. So don't let them use you." I knew I had to be tough to stay there so I was.

My sister was getting ready to move to another part of New York because the gangs were getting very bad and she didn't want me to be caught up in it. Before we moved, I saw one of the worst rumbles between two gangs – the Viceroys and the Dragons. I had never seen a fight like that in my life before.

Let me tell you how that fight got started. This young lady named Shirley lived a block down from me but on the other side of the street. She lived on one side of the street that was run by one gang and I lived on the other side of the street run by another gang. I lived on the side of the street with the Viceroy gang and she lived on the side of the street with the Dragons. Her brother, James, was one of the leaders of the Dragons.

Shirley had to go to the store one night and because I liked her I tagged along with her. On the way back from the store, one guy was walking in front of us and two were walking behind. The one in front of us was walking and doing the talking.

He said to Shirley, "Tell your brother, James, if he comes out in the street tonight he's a dead man."

Shirley said, "Why don't you tell him yourself?"

He said, "Just remember, if your brother comes out in

the street tonight – he is dead."

The two behind us never said a word.

"Who are those guys," I asked.

"They belong to the street gang called the Viceroy. They live on the side of the street where you live." Shirley said.

"No shit," I said.

Shirley picked up the pace and was walking a little faster. She got back to the house and called her mother into the kitchen. I could not overhear anything Shirley was saying to her Mother. But soon after, her mother got James in the kitchen and was talking to him. James' voice went up and I could tell he was very upset.

"No one tells me what to do. No one tells me I cannot go in the street. We will see about that," James said.

Of course, some of his friends were with him. He said, "Get the rest of the boys and meet me in the street."

His mother pleaded with him not to go in to street but that plea was in vain. That was the night that James died. He was stabbed 17 times. As the chains, the sticks and the baseball bats were swung and hit their marks, you could hear it. They yelled. I don't know how many got hurt. I think three died, others had lots of broken bones. I don't know how many were stabbed. I stayed across the street and watched it all. That was the worst I have ever seen. I will always remember this scene as long as I live. What they were fighting for I don't know. Gangs' fighting is just terrible and usually senseless.

MOVING TO THE WEST SIDE BY YANKEE STADIUM

My sister said, "I'm getting you out of here."

It wasn't long before we moved to the west side up around the Yankee Stadium. I went to George Washington High School. It was no better here. I joined the football team, the baseball team – any team to keep me out of the street.

I met this cool kid whose name was Shadrach but we called him "Shad." His twin's name was Meshach. We had fun with that name. I knew right away to stay out of the gangs. I had to join a gang but the gang I joined was a baseball team and a football team. That was my gang.

One night coming home from school, some boys took my shoes. It was snowing that night. Four guys came up to me at the bus stop and said they liked my shoes and wanted them. One held me down and the other one took them. The next day, I told Shadrach what had happened and he said it will not happen again. The boys went to the same school as I did. Now we had to find them on the schoolyard. It took some time but we found them because we were on the same football team. We went to the principal and told him what had happened. When the boys were called into the office, they denied taking my shoes.

The principal said, "If it happens again I will kick you out of this school."

On the school grounds, I was called tattletale. After

that, I never had any trouble with those boys.

I became a star wide receiver and that was my goal – to play football. Then summer comes along and it was baseball. My coach, Tiger Williams, worked with me to help me learn how to hit left-handed. I'm normally a right-handed hitter, but the curve ball from a right-handed pitcher was giving me a lot of trouble. So he worked with me and helped me learn how to hit left-handed. Now I am a switch hitter. It took me some time before I got it. It took a lot of work. I was frustrated a lot but I hung in there. That's how I became a switch hitter. I think all kids should learn how to switch hit if you're going to play baseball.

My coach's son's name was Jack. Jack was a pitcher and he worked long days to help me learn how to hit left-handed. He would throw balls after balls. His dad would look to see what I was doing wrong then he would correct me. You're not looking at the ball, Eugene. See the ball until you hit it. I was pulling my head off the ball. He would always say don't move your head. When you swing, see yourself hitting the ball.

Henry Sumpter was a little crafty left-hander. He would throw to me as I hit right-handed and Jack Williams would throw to me when I hit left-handed. I would get so mad at myself some time because if someone else can do this so can I. That is what frustrated me the most. After a lot of hard work, switch hitting paid off.

My baseball team was a good team. The football team

was another story. The Fordham Wildcats – we were anything but Wildcats.

JOINING A BAND

I knew a kid named John Darby. He was the lead singer for Pete Cook. They were looking for a backup singer. So I was asked if I would like to try it. Pete Cook played lead guitar, his son played bass guitar; his daughter played piano, and Pete was looking for lead singer – a woman to be exact. I walked into the studio and watched them practice to see if I wanted to sing backup with them. That was cool as I had never been in the studio before. Another group was working out also.

A Spanish man named Angel Angelo. He was also looking for a backup singer. So I listened to those two groups for a while. Then I decided to join Pete Cook and the Firelighters. Two brothers were with this group, Earl and Lorenzo. They couldn't go on stage unless they had a bottle of whiskey with them. They had to be drunk out of their minds before they could get on stage. I didn't care for that. We stopped the music a lot because they came in wrong. Some time they'd forget the words of the song; sometimes singing one key when we played another.

And the straw that broke the camel's back with me was when drummer, Carl, was told that I had gotten a letter from his girlfriend whose name was Johnny Mae.

I had gotten a letter from a Johnny Mae alright but this was a girl who lived in Georgia and not his girlfriend. So he invited me out to the parking lot to have it out with me. Lucky for me I had the letter in my pocket to show him. It was not from his girlfriend but another girl named Johnny Mae.

I quit the group after that and started singing backup for Angel Angelo. That was the best thing that happened because Angel was a security guard at the studio. So we got the studio to practice anytime we wanted. Earl and Lorenzo from Pete Cook had a big blow out in the parking lot and Pete was not able to practice there anymore. I was glad of that because then I didn't have to see them anymore. John Darby continued to be the lead singer for Pete Cook and the Firelighters.

I didn't know if I was going to have trouble with Pete Cook because I wrote this song called "Why can't I understand." That's the song I wrote by myself. It will always be my song. The one that I wrote with the group that is the group's song "Let one hurt do." That's the song that we all worked on together. Al Randall made a song that sounds just like it but there's nothing we could do. When we are all in a studio and listen to each other's songs, it is easy to steal from one another.

Angel decided that we would no longer write our own material but sing other people's songs like James Brown, BB King, and Sam Cook's. That way nobody could steal from us. That was a good idea. I walked into the studio one day and found my friend, Shadrach sitting there. He wanted me to come and have dinner with him at his house. I said, "Is your brother going to be there – the one with the funny name?" We laughed. He said, "Of course, he's going to be there – my brother with the funny name." I liked him and he knew it but I was just having a little fun with his name, Meshach.

"Eugene, if you become a big star would you still hang around with us?" Shadrach asked.

I replied "Shad, I will never become a big star. But if I do, I will still hang around with you. But you and I are going to play football." "What about that baseball player in New York by the name of Willie Mays. That's another person that I would like to be like. Maybe if I don't make it as a football player maybe I could play baseball."

Shad said, "You have to be a better hitter than you are now."

"Yea, Shad, I know" I said

"Who's the cutie on the piano?" Shadrach asked

"That is Pete's daughter. She is sitting in with Angel Angelo group – the group that I am with." I replied.

"Are you turning me on to her?" Shadrach asked

"Yes, man, anything for you." I said

"Well let's do it," he said.

I strolled over to the piano and Shadrach was right behind me. Mary gave Shadrach an odd look.

"Mary," I said, "I want you to meet my friend, Shadrach. Shadrach, this is Mary."

He stuck his hand out and she took it. "Glad to meet you," she said. "Likewise," Shadrach replied. And I walked away and left them alone. I found out later she thought he was crazy. I said to Mary later that I would never introduce her to any of my crazy friends. She said, thank you.

MOVING OUT OF MY SISTER'S HOUSE

I remember the day that I moved out of my sister's house and into my own home. Buying pots and pans to do my own cooking – I was now on my own. I was still with this band as a backup singer plus driving cab. My sister was not happy for me to be on my own and no brother to cook for. I bought a lot of secondhand stuff to fill my apartment because this was my home now and not my sister's place. That was strange because I had never been on my own before. Scratching my head, thinking about what I needed to buy for my apartment. Most apartments in New York are furnished but you still needed pots and pans. So after work every night I took my tip money to buy something for my apartment.

My place was like a boarding house with other people living in the building. We had to share the place together downstairs. In the basement were a washer and dryer that the whole building used. When I moved in the building there was no heat; sometimes no hot water. I said to myself that's why I got this place so cheap. How long was this going to last?

Across from me was a woman who had a son named George. Since his mom worked all day, George just sat around and played loud music. I remember getting up one morning and it was cold. I was awakened from the sound of loud music and Puerto Ricans who were always working on those damn cars. I dragged myself out of bed, took my clothes to the wash downstairs and asked George why do you have to play your music so loud?

"What did you say?" he said to me.

"Why do you have to play your music so loud," I said. He shrugged his shoulder and turned the volume down just a little. I said, "Thanks," and walked past him.

BEING A NEW YORK CITY CAB DRIVER

Since the band wasn't something that I could make a living on, I started driving cab. That way I could also send some money to my Mother in South Carolina to help her out. Imagine – being a New York City cab driver.

Because I was the newbie in the world of driving cab I took all the crappy hours from 4 pm to midnight and sometimes 12 until eight in the morning. No one who'd been with the cab company for a long time wanted to work all of the crappy hours. One night as I was sitting around waiting for my cab to come in I listened to some of the men telling stories about what had happened to them. Most of them were young men like me who had to work the crazy hours to make a living. I remember one night it was very cold and the windows on my cab didn't go all the way up so I froze my tail off. But when I worked in the summertime, the air-conditioner didn't work and that's when you found out what New York City smells like.

There are many stories about being a New York City cab driver – here are just a few.

PELHAM ONE TWO

A friend of mine named, Leonard, came by because he wanted to talk to me. I met him when he was my mailman. He had gotten a job with the railroad and worked for the transit authority in New York. His first job was working on the Pelham train. The Pelham Subway train ran from upstate New York all the way through Brooklyn at the end of the line. At this time in the '60's, the Pelham train picked up all of the money for sure from Harlem and maybe all along the route. Leonard dated a lady named Bernadette.

I was washing my clothes when Leonard told me about some people in Brooklyn who wanted him to bring a cab driver to a party. I didn't like Brooklyn so I asked Leonard why a cab driver needed to come to this party. He didn't seem to know. I said the last time I was in Brooklyn the kids said if you ever come back over here we'll send you back in a box. That's why I had never gone back to Brooklyn.

"How did you meet these people," I asked Leonard.

"They all work with me on the transit subway and they want to know someone who drives a cab," he said. He looked at me with a puzzled look.

"And that's all you know?" I asked.

"Yeah," he said. I continued to fold my clothes.

"When is this party going to take place?" I asked.

"Saturday night," Leonard said.

"What time will I meet you?" I asked.

"If you can be on the platform at your station on Prospect Avenue around 7 p.m. and when you see the train come in, if you don't see me waving my hand at you don't get on the train but wait for the next one," he said. That was my instruction.

And that's how we left it until Saturday night. Now it is Saturday night around 6:30, I walked over to the train station and waited on the platform. The first train came in and Leonard was not on that train. The second train came in; he was not on that train. The third train came in and there he was. He stepped off the train, waved his hand at me to get on and so I did.

I walked through the train following Leonard up to the car where he was with a woman who worked with him. He introduced her but I forgot her name. And off to Brooklyn we went. After arriving in Flatbush (a suburb of Brooklyn), we got off the train. He walked over to the phone booth and made a phone call. (Yes, they had phone booths on the street then – no cell phones!) We stayed in the train station until three guys came over to take us back to the apartment. There were a lot of people in the apartment that worked with him who were drinking beer, smoking pot and passing it around. I said, "No, thank you."

"A couple hits off of this will wake you up," he said.
I said, "I'm not asleep." He thought I was being smart but I wanted to have a clear head because I didn't know what I was getting myself into.

And then the guy with the sandy brown hair spoke up. He looked at me under his glasses and said, "Are you the cab driver?" I said, "Yes."

"Tell me something about you," he said.

"What do you want to know?" I asked.

"Before I tell you what we want, we have to know something about you," he said.

"Like what?" I asked.

"Is your mother alive?" he asked.

Right away that struck a nerve. "What does my mother have to do with this?" I asked.

"Just trying to get to know you." he said.

"Leonard, who is this guy? You brought us a guy who won't tell us about himself."

I replied, "You are not asking me about me, you're asking me about my mother and my father and I don't tell anyone about my mother and father."

"Then we can't use you." he said.

"Well, then I am out of here." I said.

The lady that was with us said if you're leaving then I am too.

That was an odd feeling for me because those people in Brooklyn didn't like me anyway. The little guy who was asking all the questions went to the kitchen and started talking to some of his friends. I didn't know what was said but I heard one of them say to walk us back to the subway.

Back on the subway, the lady and I were trying to figure out what was going on but couldn't come up with anything. All the way back to the Bronx nothing made sense. A cab driver and a woman who worked for the subway – what were we supposed to do. I asked her what her job was. She was a switchboard operator. A switchboard operator and a cab driver – we couldn't figure it out. It was a long ride back and still nothing came to mind.

And then I was one-stop from getting off and I told her I would walk her home but I didn't even know her and I didn't want to get into any trouble with her boyfriend.

"I don't have a boyfriend," she said.

I said, "That's strange."

She smiled and said, "What's so strange about that?"

I said, "OK – I'll walk you home then." We walked up to her apartment and a few other people in the street said hi. She lived on the second floor of her building.

"I have a friend and if he comes out he won't hurt you," she said with a grin on her face.

"What kind of a friend is this?"

"You will see."

We entered the apartment and right away she dropped-down and looked under the couch. I thought what could this be? She got glasses out of the cabinet and said, "White or red." I just waved my hand. She poured wine in both glasses and handed one to me. I start sipping my wine and out of the corner of my eye I see this snake like thing coming into the living room. It came slithering out like an old person weaving back and forth. It was time for me to go. No wonder you don't have a boyfriend. She says, "He won't hurt you."

"I know he won't because I am gone." I was out of there.

I saw Leonard a week later he said to me, "You know what those people wanted?"

"No, but you are going to tell me," I said.

Leonard said, "They were thinking about robbing the train that we work on."

"You have got to be kidding me," I said in shock.

"No, I am not. The lady that left with you was a switchboard operator and you were the cab driver," he said.

I asked, "Now will you tell me how that was going to work?"

Leonard explained, "Well, Gino (some people use to call me Gino), you would park your cab by the train station where the man was coming out of the train with the money. You would put your off-duty sign on so they would know that was the cab that they were going to get into and you would then take them to the place where they were going to divide the money."

To make that work, everyone had to be on board – the switchboard operator to the cab driver and to the crew that worked on the train. They had brought guns from Florida. Some of them were going to handcuff themselves to the middle pole on the train to make it look like they weren't involved. On the last stop before the train came from underground that's where I was to park my cab put my off-duty sign on and wait for the crew to come from underground with all of the money and then drop them off. I was never told where that last stop was because I was not a part of the plan.

"You guys have got to be crazy – a cab driver and a switchboard operator?"

"She was going to call and say there was a chain gang that was working on the track so the police would not come and disturb you."

"You are telling me all the people in that room were going to rob the train that you work on?"

"You have got to be nuts and you tried to get me into this?" I said.

Leonard said, "Gino, I didn't know. They never told me what was going on."

I looked down at my hand I didn't know whether to hit Leonard or not. People get themselves in all kinds of trouble by hanging out with other people. People that I didn't know were planning to pull off a robbery and were going to use me for their getaway. Leonard could see I was not pleased.

I was afraid to tell the story to anyone because later they made a movie about people robbing that same train. It scared the crap out of me because somebody told that story along the way. I thought that's why they made that movie, "The Taking of Pelham one two." In the movie, Walter Matthau, with a few of his friends, robbed that train. As I was watching that movie, I said to myself someone told the movie people what the potential robbers had planned. I thought because I didn't go along with it maybe they would think I was the one that squealed on them.

I never saw the lady with the snake again. I never saw the sandy hair guy that planned it all. The only person I saw again was Leonard. Bernadette moved away with him. I tried to locate him twice when I was in New York but I could not find him.

CAUGHT IN THE MIDDLE OF RIOTS

Before I picked up my cab one night, I was told by some people not to work Harlem today because there were going to be riots. I knew that beforehand because some Muslim men by the name of Earl and Lorenzo told me. They were two brothers who were in a band with me. But when I picked up my third trip sure enough they were going to Harlem. When we got into the Harlem area, there were people setting cars on fire, smashing windows, and looting like I had never seen before. The police were beating people with clubs.

It all started because of the Muslim, Elijah Muhammad, who had a lot of wives. Some other story was swirling around that he had wanted the men to leave their women with him. He had a lot of wives already. Louis Farrakhan was his right-hand man. At the time, I couldn't believe the people were destroying the city and I was caught in it.

I was also caught in a blackout. I liked driving during those times because people had no other way to get around so driving was fine as a cab driver in the blackout. Some people said they had to walk from New York to Brooklyn and across the Brooklyn Bridge. That was scary. Not for me, but for those who had to do that.

THE PICKUP FROM LAGUARDIA

I remember one night, I had picked up a man from LaGuardia Airport and he wanted to go to 59th street. As he got into my cab, I noticed he was dressed real nice and had a pinky ring on his little finger. I said to myself he was a wise guy because wise guys always wear rings on their pinky finger. He said to me "I will show you how to get in the block."

I got to the street and made a left turn. We went to the corner of the block and made a right turn. We came back and made another right turn back into a block. He said, "Park behind the cab up front." So I did. The man in the cab in front of us got out of the cab and came back and opened the door for the man in my cab. He gave me a $20 bill and said keep the change. I watched the two of them walk toward the building. I put my off-duty sign on and drove back to the cab station near Yankee Stadium where I worked. That was my work for the night.

The next night I went to work and my boss, Fred, called me into his office. There were two other men in the office with him that I wasn't introduced to. Fred pulled out my trip sheet from the night before and handed it to me. He said, "Tell me about the last man you picked up last night."

One of the men was standing with hands in his back pocket and leaned up against the wall. The other guy had his arms folded and I could tell he was studying me. Fred said again to tell me about that last guy you picked up. I didn't know what to tell.

"Was he nervous?" he asked.

"I don't know whether he was nervous." I said.

"Did he say anything?" Fred asked.

I went over the story again. I picked him up at LaGuardia Airport. He wanted to go to 59th St. so that's where I took him. He said to make a left turn into the block. So I made a left turn into the block. At the end of the street, he told me to make a right turn. So I made a right turn. We got back to the 59th St. where he said to make a right turn. I made another right turn. So we just circled the block. As we pulled back into the block, there was a cab ahead of us. He said to pull in behind that cab. So I did. The man from the cab in front come back to my car and opened the door for the guy who was in my car. He gave me $20 and said keep the change. I put my off-duty sign on and drove back to the cab station near Yankee Stadium, turned my money in and went home.

They kept hammering me about the man in my cab. I was getting a little tired of those two so I snapped at him and said, "What is going on?"

"You were the last one to see this man alive He had his head blown off." he said.

I said, "The person that blew his head off was the last one to see him alive."

The man that was standing with his hands in his pocket slammed his hand on the desk and said, "You little wise ass. If we can find you they can find you!"

I snapped back at him, "Who is they."

"Look pal," he said.

"Now I am your pal?" I said.

"You see how easy it is for us to find you then they can find you too." He said.

I said again to him, "Who is they?"

He said, "Just tell us what the other guy looked like,"

"He looked old just like the guy that was in my cab," I said.

"Did he have a fancy ring on his finger?"

"I didn't notice." I said.

"But you noticed that about the guy in your cab?"

"Yes, because he was in my cab," I said. "I didn't kill this guy."

"We didn't say you did but you could help us out and maybe we can find the other guy. If you find out anything else anything at all will you tell your boss?" One of the men said.

"Yes," I said.

To tell a guy that the last person he picked up last night was killed gangland style was enough to scare the crap out of you. The mob doesn't let anybody testify against them and I was not about to. I was jumpy all night long after my shift was over and was afraid to go home. I didn't want them following me that's how scared I was. I didn't tell the story to anyone other than my family. My brother had told me if they were policeman they would have shown me a badge. But they didn't show me a badge at all so who were they if they were not policemen? Were the two men in the office with Fred the gangsters trying to find out what I know? But I didn't know anything.

PICKING UP THE LADY AT MACY'S

Let me tell you about one of the times I got robbed. I picked up a young lady at Macy's department store and she was going to Brooklyn. She was dressed up real nice.

She said to me, "Cabby, I'm going to Brooklyn. My husband will be there to pay the cab."

Off to Brooklyn we went with all of her bags. After arriving in Brooklyn to the address she said, "Blow your horn." She sat in the backseat of my cab looking around for her husband.

She said, "Blow your horn again." And so I did. There was no husband.

She said, "Bad ass hole. I'll go inside and get your money." She got out; left all her bags in the backseat. So I figured she'd be back.

She went inside the building and that was the last time I saw her. I just got robbed. All the clothes in the backseat were the stuff that she wore before she bought the new ones she had on and probably stole.

THREE KIDS WITH SHOOTING

Another time I got robbed I was in the Bronx on the Concorde Boulevard. I picked up two black kids. I said, "Are you going to close the door?" One of them said we are waiting on our friend. And then I heard "Bam Bam". Gunshots.

The third person came and jumped into the cab – "Let's go let's go." And then "Boom". A return shot from the other guy. The three kids lay on the floor in the backseat as I took off. Of course, I couldn't lie on the floor because I had to drive the cab.

I got to the first corner and made a right turn. I know

they couldn't shoot around a corner. They said, "Where the hell are you going? Just drive." They finally told me the address.

The two kids that got in first got out and gave the third kid their money. Then he told me his address. As I pulled away from the curb to go where he wanted to go, he jumped out of the cab with all the money. I got robbed again!

GETTING KICKED

I picked up an Asian guy on 42nd St. and he wanted to go to Chinatown. He had on a Hawaiian shirt, dark glasses and a short haircut. When I pulled up to the address he gave me, I saw that he was asleep in the backseat. So I woke him up. He put his hand in his pocket and he looked around.

He said, "This isn't what I told you."

I said, "You told me East Broadway Chinatown. This is East Broadway Chinatown. Where do you want to go?"

Then I saw a police car so I flagged them down and told them what was going on. One of the cops said it is two blocks from here and if he doesn't pay you bring him back over here to us.

So I drove two blocks. He got out and reached his hand into his pocket as if he was looking for money. I rolled down my window to get paid but instead he grabbed me around the throat. He was squeezing me so hard I could hardly breathe. Then I jammed my front door into him. As I got out of the cab, he did a spinning kick hitting me in the groin. Down I went. He knocked all the air out of me and started yelling "the nigger got a gun, the nigger got a gun!"

My right arm went limp. I had no feeling in my right arm and my groin swelled up. Somehow I made it to the hospital. Unfortunately, they had to remove one of my testicles because it swelled up so big and was damaged.

TWO LADIES WITH THE BRIEFCASES IN CENTRAL PARK

Another time I picked up two black ladies and took them to Central Park. As we pulled into the Park, one of the women said to turn your meter off because you are taking us back. The lady that did the talking got out of my cab; put a briefcase on the hood of my car. As a woman approached from another cab she put her briefcase on my car and flipped it open. The two ladies examined the cases. The woman in the car with me had her hand jammed in a brown bag.

I could not see what was in the briefcases but the two ladies exchanged briefcases then she got back in the cab with me.

She said, "Cabby, take me back to where you picked us up." I pulled out of Central Park and went back to 28th Street. As the two ladies in my cab examined the briefcase, I was trying to see what was going on by looking into my mirror.

She caught me and said, "Cabby keep your damn eyes up front."

The woman who stayed in the cab with me said to me, "What time do you get off tonight?"

I said, "Midnight."

She shuffled in the bag she had. With her right hand she pulled out a pen and a piece of paper and she jotted down a phone number, handed it to me and said, "Call me when you get off."

I put it in my shirt pocket and drove on. As the two of them got out of the cab, she said, "Don't forget to call me." They gave me a good tip and I said I would call when I get off.

And so I did, but to my surprise the voice on the other end of the phone said "Sgt. Mallory speaking." I just hung up. She gave me the police number – not her number. I said damn black lady.

THE BELLEVUE HOSPITAL PICK UP

I remember one night I dropped off a person at Bellevue Hospital. There was a guy standing on the curb dressed up in a suit who wanted a cab so he got in my cab. I said to him where are you going?

He said, "Just drive."

I said to him, "Drive where? Uptown or Downtown."

He was not making any sense so I put my flashing light on to let the cops know I had a problem. As the two of us went back and forth about where he was going, the light on the top of my cab was flashing and that means I have a problem. So there came a flashing light behind me. It was the police. I pulled over and stopped.

One of the cops asked, "What's going on?"

I said, "I picked this man up at Bellevue Hospital and he won't tell me where he is going."

The cops said, "Where did you pick him up?"

"At Bellevue Hospital," I said.

The cops went back to his car got on the radio and a few minutes later he came back to my car, pulls the door open and grabs the guy by the arm. He pulls him out of my car and the cop said, "He dressed up in the Doctor clothes and walked out of the hospital."

The guy was nuts. He was in the nuthouse in the psych ward. He went in the doctor's lounge, dressed up in the doctor's suit and walked out of the front door and got into my cab. The policeman put handcuffs on him and took him back to the psych ward. That night it was time for me to go home.

I had enough. Yes, I had enough.

MY LAST CAB DRIVE

On August 28, two black females stabbed me over $14. Yes, they robbed me. My morning started out quietly by pulling my cab out of the cab station by Yankee Stadium. I stopped at a stand to buy some fruit so I could have something to eat as I drove.

Two black ladies on the street were together and one

of them said to me, "My friend is in a lot of pain. Will you take us to a doctor?"

I felt sorry for them. The woman who was talking to me helped her friend into the back seat. She sat right behind me and then the other woman ran around and got in the front seat with me. I should have known that in the middle of a hot summer, a woman wouldn't be wearing a long, heavy overcoat.

She said, "Make a right turn at the corner and I will show you how to get to the doctor office."

And so I did. As we were going, she said to me, "Not this block but the next one make a left turn."

And so I did. It was right into an alley. I knew I was in trouble because there was no doctor's office and I felt the shotgun put behind my right ear. They said give us your money. I gave them what I had. She said, "Just to show you we are not playing around."

She stabbed me in the left knee. All I had was $14.

"That's all the money I have," I said.

She said, "Where's the rest of your money?"

"That's all the money I have. You are my first customer." I said.

"Come on man, where's the money?" the one who was in the front seat with me said.

The one in the back put the hammer back on the shotgun.

"I am telling you, that's all the money that I have," I pleaded.

She took the knife and stabbed me in the left leg. Sweat rolled down my face. "Come on man," she said, "we are not playing. Where's all the money?"

"I am telling you that's all the money that I have," I said.

Somehow they must have believed me because they got out of the cab.

I took my shirt off and wrapped it around my leg and then drove myself to the hospital. I walked into the hospital and grabbed the receptionist and wouldn't let her go. She was calling out to get this man off her. He's bleeding all over the place. The next thing I know, I woke up in a hospital with my arms strapped down to the bed. The doctor told me they gave me a shot to take me off the receptionist.

I found out later I must've taken the meter out of the cab and put it in the trunk. I don't remember doing that. My boss, Fred, told me that's what I did. Another cab driver came and got my cab and took it back to the station. That's when I knew that was my last job as a cab driver.

CAB STORIES WRAP UP

For several years that was my job – driving cab. My first night on the job, someone killed the cab driver and put his body in the trunk of the car. That was my first night on the job. I would sometimes sit around and talk to cab drivers to listen to all the different stories and I said to myself is this what you want? And then you look at all the money and you said "Yes, this is what I'm going to do."

Then when the two black ladies stuck a knife in me, I knew it was time to stop. Think about it – after being shot at, robbed a few times, been in a city blackout, caught up in riots, was yelled at by two men who thought I knew something about a man who had his head blown off and was afraid to go home thinking that the man who killed that guy would come for me next. Yeah, it was time for me to stop.

There were a few good times, too. The people you pick up who give you a big tip for taking them just a few blocks. In New York City, you get the good, the bad and the ugly – it goes with the territory.

Chapter Three

MOVING TO FLORIDA & CALIFORNIA

GETTING A JOB WITH THE RAILROAD

In 1974, I moved to St Petersburg, Florida to recuperate. I had just been stabbed by two females for $14 while driving cab in New York City.

The person I moved in with was George Hurst. He was a boss for the railroad and he asked me if I would like to work for the railroad. Mr. Grey from Miami was coming down to talk with some of us about working for the railroad. Mr. Hurst told me that I must tell Mr. Grey that you always wanted to work for the railroad. Now that was a lie that I told – as I never had interest in working for the railroad.

At about the same time in 1974, they had put a freeze on hiring, because President Reagan had wanted to shut the railroad down. He didn't like the railroad and thought they were spending too much money. And Amtrak wasn't making any money. So they put a freeze on.

James Hooker who lived across the street from the Hurst family worked at Dandy Bakery. He asked me if

I wanted to try working at the bakery and so I said yes. He said he'd see what he could do to help me get a job. So he took me in and told his boss I was a good worker and I needed a job. So that's how I got the job. I worked at a bakery for about a year. That was a great experience for me. I knew how to cook but had never worked in a bakery before. I baked bread.

I had no car to go back and forth to work so I rode a bicycle to work each night. I would get on a bicycle and ride a mile and a half to Dandy Bakery each night. I got chased by dogs and got knocked off by some kid in a Volkswagen. As I rolled on the ground trying to find something to throw at them, I could hear them laughing. My hand felt a bottle and I threw it into the direction of the car. I heard one of the guys say, "Oh, shit!" and they drove away. Now I'm trying to get up off the ground and I hoped that I didn't grab a snake because Florida has a lot of snakes and gators.

As I rode my bike to work I was worried about the dark spot around the lake with no light and going under the overpass. That's where the Volkswagen knocked me off my bike. The next day I told George Hurst what had happened. So he took me down to a car lot and helped me buy a car. My first car was a blue Dodge Dart. Now I didn't have to be chased by dogs, bumped off a bike and not worry about kids in a Volkswagen.

All I did was bake bread for a year and then Amtrak took the freeze off in 1975 and started hiring again. Mr.

Grey again came down and talked with a bunch of blacks about working for the railroad.

After nine months of working at the bakery, Amtrak called and said for me to come in. George Hurst, Jr. and I both took the physical. George Hurst's other son, Tommy, and I went to see a man named Mr. Grey. Mr. Grey was the head man for Amtrak out of Miami. He was the guy who was doing all the hiring so we went in one by one to talk to him. George had told me to say I always wanted to work for the railroad. So in 1975 I got a job on a train and was first sent to culinary school in Chicago to learn how to cook. After I finished my class, I was put on a train with a crew going back and forth to Chicago. I was now a cook on the railroad.

After a year, St. Petersburg closed its crew base and all of the workers had to go to Miami, New York or New Orleans. I chose New Orleans because I didn't want to go back to New York and I didn't like Miami. I was working on the "extra board" out of New Orleans which meant you didn't have a regular run. Sometimes I went to Chicago and sometimes to Los Angeles. All of the cooks who had more seniority than I did would come in and take the jobs they liked. This meant I could lose the job that I liked. So Amtrak made me a bartender. I had never worked bartender before but I was trained. After three trips as a bartender, I went out on my own from New Orleans to Los Angeles. I liked that run.

I had heard Amtrak was planning on closing the New Orleans base office, too. About that same time, I met a man named James who ran a tennis shop in California. He asked if I could come out and help him run it. So I jumped at it. I told Amtrak I would like to move to California I didn't want to go back to Florida, because of all the storms. And I didn't want to go back to New York. The New York City life is what got me to Florida in the first place, after the two women stabbed me for $14 when I was driving cab. And in Florida, the storm season comes along and it seems like the house was going to blow down.

One day my boss called some of us into the office and said we have an opening in Los Angeles if anyone would like a transfer. I put my hand up. "Montgomery would you like to be transferred to Los Angeles?" he asked.

I said, "Yes."

He slid a piece of paper across his desk and said to sign it. They are looking for sleeping car attendants and if you are interested in moving to California, we will send you there. That's how I got to Los Angeles. It was 1978.

I bought a 1977 Pontiac Grand Prix blue-and-white, sunroof, tape deck – the works. It had everything in it. My credit union asked me why I wanted a car with all that stuff on it. I asked who is paying for this car you or me. Don't tell me what I buy with my own money. I pulled all of my money out of the credit union in Florida because of this.

As I let everyone know that I was moving to California, a woman asked me if I could let her son come along. The kid's father lived in California and wanted him to come out and work with him. She offered me gas money and said he could help me drive. He looked to be in his late 20's so I said yes.

So I put all my belongings on the train and headed to California. With a brand-new car, we got on the road at night because we wanted to be going through Texas at night because it was so hot. Two and a half days later we were in Los Angeles, California. He called back to New Orleans to say we had made it and after dropping him off I never saw him again.

I stayed at the Clark Hotel on Figaro Street in the heart

of the ghetto, the cheapest place to stay. It was a fleabag hotel. I lived on the third floor. Everyone shared the same bathroom and kitchen down the hall. There was no bathroom in the room; the lock on my door didn't work sometimes so I tried to stay on the train as much as possible so I didn't have to stay in that hotel.

I moved to California as a cook/waiter/bartender/sleeping car attendant. I didn't have a regular job. I worked on what was called the "extra board." So I had to go out whenever they called me to do whatever job was open. I worked from California to Seattle on the Coast Starlight.

An Asian man who was an Amtrak supervisor named Tony Tam said to me, "I will let you work as long as you want to until you find a better place to live." He said to just give him $35 each time.

I did 28 days on the train without having a day off. My nerves and hands would begin to shake. I was told if I didn't take some time off I was going to have a nervous breakdown.

Once they sent me out as a waiter. I shouldn't have taken that job as I spilled a tray of spaghetti on a passenger's head. That was my most embarrassing time ever working on the train. Everybody teased me for a long time and still do. So I got out of waiting tables!

Chapter Four

TRAIN STORIES

PASSENGER KICKED OFF TRAIN – "CAN YOU FLY?"

I was a lounge attendant at this time from LA to Seattle, WA on the Coast Starlight. A passenger came into the bar and wanted a six-pack of beer. I sold him a six-pack and he went back upstairs (because the snack bar was on the first level of the train).

The conductor came down and said I want you to go and find out what that guy you just sold the six-pack to is doing with it. So I went upstairs and I see that this man is giving this young girl drinks. She looked to be drunk already but he was still physically pouring beer down her throat and the beer was running down her face. I told him you can't do that and told him you're cut off. I went back downstairs and he followed me.

"What do you mean I'm cut off?" he asked.

I explained to him that that kid is drunk already and probably underage. He opened the train door and asked me "Can you fly?" The train was going about 70 miles an hour at the time. "No," I said but I asked him, "Can you fly?" He was going to throw me off the train. I slammed the door shut. I picked up the intercom and called the conductor.

I told the conductor I will not run this bar again until this man is off the train. And he told the passenger, "You are off the train at the very next stop." As the conductor walked away he followed him yelling things to him. The conductor then called the engineer and told him to call the next stop and have the police there when we get there; we're putting this guy off the train. At the next stop, the conductor came and took this man and put him off the train. He was very unhappy to say the least – but at least I didn't get thrown off the train by him.

TOILET FLUSHING PROBLEMS

We were in Denver, CO and I was working on the Pioneer from Seattle to Chicago. At a layover stop in Denver, the bathroom dumped in the station. That was the first time that had ever happened.

Another time that something similar happened was on the Coast Starlight going from Seattle to LA. We were leaving Portland and going across the bridge. Miss Portland, the beauty queen, was going under the bridge and doing her "Beauty queen" wave while she was on a boat. Someone flushed the toilet and it dumped right on top of her. You see every 100 flushes the toilet would dump out onto the track.

When Amtrak first started in the 1970's, every time you went to the bathroom it went right onto the track, in fact you could actually see the track going by when you looked down the commode.

After several instances like this, the Health Department got on Amtrak and they had to fix that problem. First it went to dumping every 100 flushes and now it goes into a holding tank where it gets pumped out at the end of the run.

TOO HOT OR TOO COLD

I got the manifest for my trip and there was a lady named Tempton. She was alone and was in Room 15 also considered the family room. That was the biggest room on the train and for her to be in it by herself seemed strange. That was coming out of LA. She went into the shower down the hall and she couldn't get the shower to turn off. She called me to turn the shower off. So I gave her more towels as there was water everywhere. Of course, I tried not to look – as she was in the shower you know.

In her room, the heat came on and she couldn't turn it off – now it's hot. The train had come to a stop and she wanted to know why the train had stopped. So I had to get the conductor to explain to her why the train had stopped. I said to myself, she must have stepped in "Pig shit" sometime in her life because it seems like everything is happening to her.

She wanted breakfast in her room the next morning. She went to bed around 11:35 pm. I thought my trouble was over and she was down for the night but it was just getting started. The room was hot again and she couldn't cool it off. My bell rang and it was her again. So I turned all the heat off in the whole car and turned the air conditioning on. Now everybody in the car is freezing because of that woman.

Now other passengers were complaining because it was too cold. So I went back downstairs and turned the heat on again. And pretty soon it was too hot.

The next morning when she got up everyone was mad. She still wanted that breakfast in her room. After bringing her breakfast, she said the food was cold. So I had to take the food back to the diner and reheat it again. That didn't make the cook happy because they were busy. And this lady was going all the way to Seattle – the whole trip.

So I asked the conductor if someone could fix my heating system. The conductor said he'd call the engineer and have them call someone. That person would be either in Klamath Falls or Portland – a place where they could fix it.

That trip went like that all the way to Seattle. I was glad to be off that train. And she told me if you're not freezing me out you're trying to burn me up – what are you trying to do to me. I don't remember if she gave me a tip or not I just wanted her off the train.

MILITARY GUY GETS FREE BOOZE

A guy got on the train in Eugene, OR. He was in the service and was going back to his base camp. That had to have been around 6:30 pm and by 11:30 or midnight the bar closed but he was still in the bar.

When the bartender came to work the next morning, this guy was still in the bar. He had broken the latch to get into the bar area, crawled across the counter and started drinking up all the liquor. He got so drunk, he passed out.

Walter Wilson was the bartender and he called the conductor who called the police. The conductor told the police that we have a military guy on the train passed out drunk. At the next stop, the military police took him off the train. They said he would be in a lot of trouble when he got back on Base. Meanwhile, the train had to sit in the station for an hour while they dealt with this guy.

BATS IN THE ATTIC

We were leaving Denver going to Chicago. There was a father and son who got on. The father was in Room 2 right across the hall from me and the son in Room 4. I put everybody's bed down leaving Denver as that was my quitting time for the night.

Sometime during the night about 2 am, I heard my bell ringing "ding dong, ding dong". It was the man in Room 2. I was stumbling trying to put my clothes on. It was kind of funny with the train rocking back and forth and me trying to get my clothes on at 79 mph. Finally, I got my clothes on and it was the guy across the hall from me.

He told me "There's bats in the attic."

I said, "There's no attic on this train."

He said "Look at me, do I look crazy to you?"

I said no, but I was thinking something else.

I could hear a little trill from up above. It sounded like when you put a baseball card in the spokes of your bicycle – it would sound like that. He told me to go get the conductor – so I did. I told the conductor what had happened.

The conductor said "There's bats in His attic."

The conductor came back to the car with me and talked with the passenger. We went downstairs and turned the air conditioner off. It was the AC that was making that noise. We told him that we got rid of the bats in the attic and he was pleased.

But the next morning, his son who had listened to the whole thing during the night told us his Dad had a stroke and sometimes he hears things like that. I thought he could have told us that before.

JALAPENO PEPPERS AND BOMBS

This was on the Empire Builder going from Seattle to Chicago. We had Room 5 that didn't get on in Seattle so the conductor could sell that room to someone on board. We got into Minot, ND they put a man back on the train because he had gotten off the train the day before because he was sick. So the conductor said they were going to put him in Room 5. I put his bed down.

The next morning, I saw him on the phone as I walked through the train. He seemed a little agitated about something but he didn't tell me what was going on but he kept talking on his phone.

Meanwhile, Amtrak got a call saying someone had called to say there was a bomb on the train. So the next stop was Portage, WI. At that stop, everybody had to get off the train. Across the street there was a school and everyone had to go there. The conductor and police told each attendant to write the passengers name and phone number on a piece of paper. We each had to take care of our own car. So this guy who was in Room 5 wrote down his name and phone number, too.

They brought the dogs on the train. They were sniffing all the baggage – carry on and checked. There was a lady going from Seattle to Michigan who happened to have fireworks in one of her bags. The dogs found that too! They thought it was the bomb – but it was those cherry bombs. Another passenger had a loaded 38 pistol in his bag on the rack where anyone could have gotten it.

The FBI said that as the train was moving they could see the caller's phone was following the train. So they knew he was on the train. So after they wrote down their phone numbers, the FBI could match his number with the one who called in. The passenger in the meantime

was trying to call the phone company to get his phone shut off. He said he had a bad reaction to the jalapeno peppers he had eaten the day before so he thought that caused him to do this.

It took five hours to go through all this. Of course, I called my wife back home to make sure she didn't hear anything about a bomb on Amtrak and to tell her I was OK.

Later I found out he was convicted of this offense – but I'm not sure on the sentence.

SEEING EYE PARROT

Many times people would try to bring unusual animals on the train. For instance a person tried to get on the train with a parrot. He told us it was a "Seeing eye parrot." We said – what does he do, tell you to go right – go left?? We didn't buy that one but because we didn't know for sure we had to let him on.

FERRET SURPRISE

Again going from Denver to Chicago, the conductor saw a passenger with a ferret about to board the train. The conductor said, "You can't bring that thing on the train." It was about a half an hour before we had to leave so he went back out on the street to try to get rid of the ferret.

He snapped at me and said "I got rid of the ferret, OK?"

I said, "I didn't say you had to get rid of it – the conductor did."

He walked upstairs and went into his room. All the passengers' beds were already down. About two in the morning I heard a woman screaming. The ferret was in her bed and it was scratching and biting her as she was trying to get it out of her bed.

So I went to get the conductor to take him to the room of the guy that was supposed to have gotten rid of the ferret. He told the conductor "I got rid of the ferret."

The conductor said, "What did he do follow you back to the train?" But who else had a ferret.

The police had to take him in because the woman was scratched up pretty good and we didn't know if the ferret had rabies or not.

NATIVE AMERICAN TRIBES HAVE AN UPRISING

Another Amtrak employee and I went from LA to Deming, NM to meet the train coming from New Orleans because the attendant from that train got sick and they needed someone to make up the beds. When we got to Deming, the ticket agent said that for our safety they would lock us up in the train station because the two different Native American tribes in the area were having a disagreement. They wanted to keep us safe.

Just imagine being locked in a station and not knowing whether the building would be put on fire or who knows what. We were there by ourselves as the ticket agent went home. He came back a half hour before the train came into the station. We never saw any uprising but it was still scary just the same.

MEETING MARTHA STEWART
AND OTHER CELEBRITIES

I went to work one day on Train #7, the Empire Builder which was my regular run going from Seattle to Chicago. I was in car #730 the one right next to the diner. When I went in to pick up my timesheet and manifest, my boss had taken it in his office because he wanted to see me.

First thing I thought was that I was in trouble and someone had complained about me. So I went into his office not knowing what I was being confronted with.

As I walked into his office, he got up and shook my hand and gave me the manifest to look at. I looked at it and put it back down. He said, "Do you see who's riding with you?" I picked it up and looked again.

I saw that Martha Stewart was getting on in Minneapolis/St.Paul. Then he was telling me how I should make sure to put on a clean shirt. That was insulting because I always put on a clean shirt. I had been with the company over 20 years by that time. I didn't think he needed to tell me that.

When I got to the train, there were four people in the car cleaning it. And they were paying special attention to Bedroom E – the room that Martha Stewart was supposed to be in. They were putting in flowers, cheese and crackers and bottle of wine and anything else they could think of.

I said, "I wish Amtrak would do this for all its passengers and not just for Martha Stewart."

Then the conductor got on the train at the station and went through the same ordeal – clean shirt, etc. All along the route, they changed conductors and with every conductor they all had the same questions and instructions. Each conductor was telling me how I was suppose to act which by now really got me "Fried."

Now we are pulling into Minneapolis/St.Paul two days later. The station supervisor was walking along the outside of my car. The train came to a stop, the supervisor helped me unload and get rid of all the garbage. He said to me, "Martha Stewart is getting on your train today. Did you know that?" I said, "Yea, I've been hearing that all the way across country."

After unloading my passengers, I started receiving passengers. A cab pulled up to my car. Out stepped this lady who said she was in Bedroom E. I looked at her and I looked at the name on my manifest – and neither one seemed to match up to the Martha Stewart I knew. But that was her name!

Boy was Amtrak fooled and what a fuss for someone that they thought was special. I said again, "Why don't they treat all their passengers the way they treated this 'Martha Stewart?'"

This person didn't turn out to be the celebrity everyone thought she was; however, there were many celebrities I met on the train. I met John Travolta who traveled when he was working on "Look Who's Talking." Then there was Whoopi Goldberg going from LA to San Francisco. Others were Pat Benatar, JoAnne Whorley (from Laugh In), Cybil Sheperd, Pearl Bailey, Ed Luther, John Madden (who taught be how to play polish poker), and Barbara Hale (from the Perry Mason Show). You just never know who you will meet on the train.

Chapter Five

EXCITING TIMES IN CALIFORNIA

STARTING MONTY IMPORT/EXPORT BUSINESS

I was still living in the Clark Hotel during all this time. Living in the Clark Hotel was as bad as living on the street.

Then I met a man named Bob Johnson. He came by my room on the train one day. We were on our way to Chicago. He said, "Monty do you want to go to breakfast?"

I went downstairs in my car, picked up the intercom and told everyone in my car I was going to breakfast and if they needed anything let me know now before I leave. No one wanted anything so I went to breakfast. While we were having breakfast Mr. Johnson said. "You live in a fleabag motel. You have got to get out of there, and I will show you how."

He said "What do you do when you get to Chicago?"

I said, 'I change my clothes go downstairs and have fun with the people in the bar."

Mr. Johnson said, "You're not going to do that anymore. You're going to save your money and start a business. "That just went over my head.

We arrived in Chicago and he said. "You're hanging out with me today."

We went to a restaurant around the corner from where we stayed at the Allerton Hotel. He said the people in the restaurant knew him and knew what kind of wine he drank. They sat a bottle of wine on the table when he came in there. He told them that I was "Monty." After dinner, he came to my room and he told me to get the pad out by the dresser by the bed. He asked me my name.

I said. "Mr. Johnson, you know my name."
He said "Just tell me what I asked you." He said, "You're going to take your money and start a business." – again, that went right over my head. What kind of business.

He said "What do people call you?"

I said, "Monty."

He said, "Then you're going to call it Monty Import/Export."

I asked, "What am I importing?"

He said, "Nothing".

What am I exporting?

He said, "Nothing. It's just a name of a business."
He asked me, "How much money do you have in your pocket?"

I said, "$272."

He said, "Tomorrow morning, I want you to show me $272 when we meet for breakfast."

That would mean that I didn't go downstairs to throw

away my money. That was the longest night for me sitting in the hotel room with money in my pocket and not going downstairs to spend it with my friends.

The next morning, he knocked on the door. It was Mr. Johnson. He said, "Show me $272."

I counted it out to him. Then he knew I didn't go downstairs to throw my money away. We went to breakfast that morning, got back on train 4. When we got back to LA, I had about $500 in my pocket. He walked me across the street to the Government building. We walked upstairs and there was a black lady there who waited on me. I started Monty Import/Export business and Mr. Johnson helped me do the paper work.

My business license cost $68.

"Now go and put some money in the bank under Monty Import/Export, he said. He told me there was a place I could get business cards printed up. It didn't cost much. He took me down to the garment district and showed me around. That's when I started buying crate loads of jeans.

A man by the name of Art Foxal was my first customer who bought a pair of jeans from me. Then I talked to my crew members and told them what I did and asked if they would buy clothes from me. Most of them said, yes. And this is how my business started. I took all their clothes sizes down whether they bought clothes from me or not I knew their sizes. So when I went out on my next trip I took two suitcases. One was for my clothes to sell to the crew and one for my Amtrak uniforms to wear.

Then I went to the garment district by myself without Mr. Johnson. And there was a pair of Braxton jeans in the window which I had never seen before. I thought those were cool. There was a young man sitting behind the counter. A woman was off to his left. I showed him my business license.

I said, "I work for Amtrak and I'd like to buy a lot of these jeans from you."

Before he could answer, the woman spoke to him but in a different language that I didn't understand. So the two chatted back and forth as I looked on not knowing what was going on.

When he spoke to me again he said. "My mom said if I buy all my clothes from them they will give me credit."

I said, "A line of credit?"

And he said, "Yes, a line of credit."

Then we exchanged addresses and right away, he let me get $500 worth of clothes on credit. That's how I started. This went well. I asked my girlfriend at the time to come help at the store that I had just opened up near where the LA Rams played football. I was the only Black in the neighborhood with a store. The rest were Asian and White. I was doing very well in that store.

Bob said, "Now I'd like to get you out of that fleabag hotel. I know a woman who has a house with rooms to rent. I would like for you to move into her house. Her son, Nate, played in this movie "Enter the Dragon" with Bruce Lee. So he moved out and was now living in Hollywood. I will take you by to see her tomorrow." It kind of brought tears to my eyes that this old man wanted to help me. I could not let him down. After stopping off at the Clark motel to put my stuff away, I asked myself what in the hell are you doing here – the door on my room didn't work well, all the street people running in and out of the building. With the money I was making this was one of my low points. I knew I had to get out of there.

The next day as I was sitting in my room, there was a knock on my door. It was Bob Johnson who wanted to take me to see Ruby Johnson who had a room to rent. So he told me where to meet him and we went to see Mrs. Johnson. I followed Bob over to Mrs. Johnson's house. The two Johnson's were not related. Mrs. Johnson was working in the front yard. I had a good feeling right away about her. She was about the size of my mother. Every time she talked, her hands had to move – just like my Mom. Bob introduced us and told her that I was living in a fleabag hotel downtown – the Clark Hotel. She looked at me and said, "Honey, you got to get out of there. I have two rooms to rent. Do you want one of them?" So I jumped at the chance and moved out of that fleabag hotel.

COOL BREEZE

I had also opened up a shop to sell my clothes. One

day I was in my shop, a man walked in. He was about 10 or 15 lbs heavier than me. He had a cane and a limp in his walk.

He asked me, "Do you own this establishment?" He had some kind of accent.

I said, "Yes, I do."

He said his name was Cool Breeze. I asked what kind of a name is that.

He said, "You making fun of my name?"

I said, "No."

He said, "I'm the guy that looks after all the stores in the neighborhood to make sure nobody breaks their windows, etc. But you have to do something for me."

I said, "What's that?"

You need to sell some "tings" for me, he said.

I said, "What kind of "tings?" I had a bad feeling. I wasn't going to sell no "tings" in my store for nobody.

He said, "I can't help you if somebody breaks your windows."

Then I said to him. "If somebody breaks my window, I'll look for Cool Breeze."

He said – are you treatening me?'

I said, "We don't say "treaten" in this country – we say threaten."

He looked at me under his sunglasses and said "Nobody threatens Cool Breeze," and left the store. That irritated me.

Later on that day, I walked outside and I walked

down the block a couple of doors down from my store. There were two white men and a woman talking about something and as soon as I walked in they stopped. I told them who I was – that my store was down the street from them. I asked if they had any trouble with a man called Cool Breeze.

I could tell they didn't want to talk with me because they thought I was probably a part of his gang. So I told them what had happened earlier, but I could tell they still didn't want to talk with me. But after I explained to them what had happened I went back to my store. Later one of them came to my store and he told me the same story that I told them – that they had the same problem with the same guy.

GIRLFRIEND STARTS USING HEROIN

We were making so much money that I couldn't keep track of it. And that was the problem because my girlfriend started shooting heroin. Her daughter was using the store for her own shopping spree.

I told her one day that where she was living, she shouldn't be wearing clothes that short because the guys would come after her. But her mother told me to leave her alone. But one day it happened. Three boys jumped her as soon as she got off the bus right there in broad daylight. She was just high school age and going to Crenshaw High School. She refused to testify against the boys. The only way we could do anything about these guys was for her to testify but she refused. I think the gang was called the Posse.

The daughter moved back to Florida and never came back to California again.

TURMOIL AT HOME

I got off the train coming from Chicago one day. Three policemen were waiting for me at the train station. Badges were flashed in my face and with all the Amtrak people looking on they asked if I was Eugene Montgomery. They put my bags on the ground opened them up and took out my dirty laundry piece by piece and laid it on the dirty ground.

I asked him, "What is this all about?"

The guy said, "Do you have any drugs in your bag?"

That was a shocker as I don't do drugs. The cop took his baton and went up the inside of my legs.

He told me, "Your house is a shooting gallery."

I asked, "What's a shooting gallery?'

He said, "Don't tell me you don't know. Every time you leave home, your house is full of junkies. So you have to be the one bringing it in."

I was so mad because I didn't know anything about this. They left all my dirty clothes on the pavement and I had to pick them up all while my Amtrak buddies are looking on. I felt like a dime – I felt so small.

I went in the crew base and signed out and told my supervisor that I'm not going out on my next trip. I need to find out what's going on at my house.

I said, "If you want me to get a doctor's notice to do that, I'll get it."

I got home and I asked my girlfriend what was going on and she said, "You know how the police in LA are. If you're doing good they don't like that. They don't like to see Black people do good in California. They are feeding you a bunch of crap."

I said, "Somebody's feeding me a bunch of crap and I'm going to find out who."

I went out and bought myself a pump shotgun. I showed the guy at the gun store my business license, and since I had that it was no problem getting a gun and also since I didn't have a police record. For some reason, he asked, "what are you going to do with this gun?"

I said, "Hunting rabbits."

"If you're going to hunt rabbits, I need to put a plug in it so it will only shoot one bullet at a time." he said.

I said, "No, I don't want that right now. If I need it I'll come back and get it."

He showed me how to take it apart and put it back together again – which was good. So I put the shotgun in the trunk of the car so no one knew I had it. The next morning I drove to the bank to put my tips in the bank. A brown Plymouth followed me to the bank. I knew it was a detective. I called my friend, James, from the pay phone outside the shop and he said Monty you need to watch out – they're looking for something if they are following you. I said, "They followed me all the way to my store."

I opened my store and while I was doing my paperwork, two cops came in – I think it was the same two that were following me. They started flipping through my clothes.

I asked, "Can I help you guys?"

They said, "No – just looking."

Then one came to the counter and asked, if I had bought any stolen goods lately?

I said, "I don't buy any stolen goods." So I showed them my paperwork. My file cabinet was two boxes – one for buying and one for selling. So I just handed him the "Buying" box. They just looked my paperwork, handed it back to me and walked out.

HOUSE GETS SHOT UP

I lived in Englewood, CA on Englewood Avenue. This is a place north of LosAngeles near where the LA Lakers played basketball. I had an apartment on the second floor in this large house facing the street. I got off the train one day and they were fixing the driveway between the two buildings so I had to park on the street.

I got home one morning. My landlady saw me when I parked (she lived on the first floor right below me). She came out and said before you take your suitcase out of your car go upstairs and take a look at your apartment. I had been gone for a whole week so it was a lot of clothes.

So I walked upstairs and it seemed like it took forever because I didn't know what I was going to find. My door was open and not locked. There were bullet holes inside the apartment all over the place. So I looked around and checked the whole place. There was stuff broken all over, things were damaged all over from where the bullets hit.

After I carefully looked over my whole apartment I went downstairs and asked my landlady – what had happened?

Directly across the street an old lady would sit in a rocking chair every day. Her name was Ms. Williams. I saw her sitting in her rocker so I went to talk with her. She said there were three guys who pulled up in front of your place yesterday. One guy stayed behind in the car at the steering wheel, the other two got out. They took these long things and put them on the front of their car which I understand were "Clips" for guns. Then they put these long things on their guns and pumped them. Then they stood back and sprayed the apartment with bullets from the street to the second floor apartment. And she said "Oh please, God, don't let that man be in that house." She said, "They did this twice because they had two clips on the car for each of them."

This shooting was a result of my girlfriend getting involved with the wrong crowd. She was buying drugs, and doing whatever she needed to do to get support her drug habit. It was so bad that she was even shooting between her toes so there would be no marks. This also explained why she couldn't get up to open the store – she was drugged.

When I went down to the dry cleaners to pick up my clothes they weren't there. Come to find out she was selling my clothes and the clothes out of the store. She was doing this to get money for her drugs. My girlfriend went down to the dry cleaner and had a fight with them claiming they had sold my clothes. But she never even put the clothes into the cleaners. She was the biggest liar I ever knew.

The manager told me that I had to move because I was making it dangerous for people to live in that building. So I had to move.

GIRLFRIEND LEAVES

Then I found a place on Manchester Boulevard almost across the street from where the Lakers played basketball. Sometimes I would come home and if there was a game going on, I couldn't find a place to park. Sometimes they would even park in my yard and that would make me so mad. So I'd have to find a place to park three blocks down and walk home leaving my suitcase in the car because I was too tired to carry it home.

When I got into my house, I saw there was a light in the bathroom. For some reason I didn't turn on any lights inside – I just came into the house. I eased the bathroom door open and I found my girlfriend inside with a needle stuck in her arm. She wanted to know what I was doing there.

I asked, "What are you doing with a needle in your arm."

She said, "You didn't see what you thought you saw."

I know what I saw.

She started bouncing checks so I had to close the account. I got off from work one day and she was gone. I found out later from her mother that she moved to New York City. And I also found out about a month or so later that they found her with a needle in her arm in an alley way and she had enough heroin in her body to kill a horse. She never came out of that one.

LEAVING CALIFORNIA

After all this, I wanted to be out of California. I could see I was going to get killed if I stayed around. So I put in for a transfer with Amtrak. That took a while for that to come through, but eventually in 1989 I got the transfer to Seattle – where I ended my career with Amtrak after 30 years in 2005.

Chapter Six

LIFE CALMS DOWN

When I moved to Seattle, the first thing that happened was 28 straight days of rain. I thought what did I do! I was almost ready to move back to California. But it was a choice between earthquakes in California (which I hated) or rain. I stuck with the rain.

HOW I MET MY WIFE

I was working from Seattle to Chicago and back on the Pioneer train. That was the name of the train I worked on during this time.

I was leaving Chicago coming back to Seattle. My car was full from Chicago to Denver except for bedroom B which was getting on in Denver. The passenger in bedroom A didn't like his room and wanted to move to bedroom B. I told him I could not move him because the person in bedroom B gets on in Denver. He said I don't want to ride all across country backwards as that's how that bedroom was set up – to ride backwards. Bedroom B was set up to ride forward. So he wanted to move to that room. Then he asked to see the conductor.

I went to get the conductor for him. The conductor

decided to move him knowing the person in that room was getting on in Denver. The conductor's name was Bill Cartright.

I said, "Mr. Cartright, that room is getting on in Denver."

Mr. Cartright was getting off in Denver so he didn't care. After arriving in Denver, I went to see the conductor that was taking over who was Art Gilmore. I told him what had happened – that the previous conductor had moved the person from bedroom A to bedroom B. He said he'd go talk to Mr. Cartright about this matter. He said thank you for telling me.

He looked out the window and pointed and said, "See that lady? She's going to Seattle. Go out and help her with her bags."

I went to help her with her bags. She was riding in coach, but I helped her anyway. We introduced ourselves. Her name was Myla. We chit-chatted along the way and I discovered she was going out to Seattle to do a fundraiser for a non-profit organization she was involved with – Terry Home. (Terry Home provides housing for young adults who have all survived a traumatic brain injury. It is named after her nephew who survived his injury in 1984 but had no place to stay but a geriatric nursing home. Myla's family decided to build a home for Terry and other young people like him and this fundraiser was to raise money for that organization.)

Myla and I chatted along the way to Seattle. I

discovered that usually she would fly out to Seattle, but for some reason she didn't want to do that this time. So she decided to try the train. I gave her my phone number and told her to call me while she was in Seattle. She didn't.

However, when I went back out on an extra trip that Amtrak asked me to take, there she was again!! We knew God must have a plan for us. So just a little over a year later, Myla moved to Seattle and we were married in 1996.

FINDING MY BIRTH CERTIFICATE

My wife and I celebrate our wedding anniversary each year by going to White Rock, BC, Canada which is just 120 miles from where we live. When they changed the rules on what you needed to cross the border, it started a whole new adventure for us.

We now needed a passport to cross into Canada. Neither of us had ever had a passport and to get one you need a birth certificate. This sounds like an easy task and it was for Myla having been born in a hospital in Sibley, IA. However, for me it was quite different.

You see I was born in a house by a mid-wife in South Carolina. A lot of the midwives couldn't read or write and quite often they would birth several babies before they went to record it at the court house.

We tried the county seat in Orangeburg, SC with several different dates, and several different names. (Very early on my mother named me Alec – but they changed it to Eugene because they didn't want people to say I was a smart "Alec.") We called and called. We even went directly to the court house one time when we were visiting family in South Carolina. You see, at this location, there still isn't a lot that is on the computer. Most of it is still in paper copy and in the basement.

When we went to the office, they finally said, "Mr. and Mrs. Montgomery, let me tell you how we research this. We check a ten year period around the date you give us for any boy babies with that name and parents. During that time period, there were no boy babies born to Eloise and Isaac Montgomery named Eugene."

So what were we to do to get a passport? They told us if we could get three people to sign a "birth affidavit" acknowledging that they knew me when I was young and have a notary public attest to that, then those affidavits and a school record that we found would get me my birth certificate.

That's what we did. We found three people who knew me growing up, asked them to complete the affidavit and we brought those to the court house. We now have my passport, but we're still not sure if that was the actual date of my birth.

CLOSING THOUGHTS

I feel that I have led a very exciting and interesting life with lots of unusual experiences so far. It is because of these experiences, I feel very fortunate to have survived many times in my life. My wife and I often say that we think God must have really wanted us to be together because otherwise, I could have been dead at any one of these circumstances.

It is also because of these circumstances that I wanted to and continue to give back to the community.

For example, in 2001 we started a non-profit organization called Montgomery, K.O.S.S. (Keep Our Schools Safe). This organization gives train rides to young children ages 8-10 years of age if they were good for the year. As of 2016, we have given over 1,800 children train rides.

The reason we started this organization stems back to a time when I was tutoring at a local elementary school. I was in the hallway working with a little boy and his reading when another little boy came up to me and said, "Jessica needs someone to put bullets in her gun." I was so shocked I wasn't sure what to do but I told him to bring Jessica to me and I'll put the bullets in the gun.

I went and called the teacher in the room and told her what had happened. The teacher went to get another teacher from next door. She asked me to repeat the story. They said, "They don't bring guns to our school."

Then the boy and girl came around the corner, the teachers backed off so they could observe without being seen. I asked, "Are you Jessica?" She didn't answer, she looked at me, and she looked at the teachers. I said, "If you want me to put bullets in your gun you have to give me the gun." I could see she was thinking about it. She took the backpack off her back, put it between her legs and then she unzipped the backpack. She pulled the gun gingerly out of the backpack like she was afraid of it. The teachers' mouths dropped open.

She pulled it out and put it on the table. I said, "Where are the bullets?" Jessica reached in her pocket and pulled out a hand full of all kinds of bullets. I said, "Holy chriminy, how many guns do you have at your house?"

The teachers came and asked what was going on. Jessica said that some little boy was pulling her pony tail

on the bus and during school and that made her mad. Her classmates were teasing her and saying "Jessica has a boyfriend, Jessica has a boyfriend." That really made her mad. So she thought she would just shoot this little boy and then her trouble would be over. I told her, "If you don't shoot this little boy, I'll give you a ride on the train." That did the trick.

Of course, I had to start giving train rides which I did one at a time. But that was the basis for the Montgomery KOSS program. Each year we still continue to give train rides and donations are always welcome!

There are other ways that I give back to the community. I volunteer often at Terry Home (the home for Traumatic Brain Injury survivors), at our church in NE Tacoma cooking for the Men's breakfast and other events. I also volunteer at coaching tennis at a local high school.

I also enjoy my writing class, playing pickleball, rock collecting and tumbling and turning them into jewelry and attending Art Shows, and embellishing lamps and vases. All of this keeps me busy and off the streets at night. And I think it helps to keep me young.

Since I have survived Non-Hodgkin's lymphoma twice and now a stem cell transplant, I feel very fortunate for everything that I've been able to do. I look forward to each day with enthusiasm.

My motto is: Cancer is just a bump in the road for a guy who likes to go fast.